Mastering the Job Interview

The MBA Guide to the Successful Business Interview

Alexander Chernev

Kellogg School of Management
Northwestern University

2006 Edition

Mastering the Job Interview: The MBA Guide to the Successful Business Interview

Second Edition | August 2005

ISBN 0-9763061-2-3

www.InterviewToolbox.com

Acknowledgements

I would like to thank the Career Management Center at the Kellogg School of Management at Northwestern University for the input in writing this book. I would also like to thank the administration of the Kellogg School of Management for providing support for my research and teaching activities.

I am also grateful to students in the executive and MBA programs at the Kellogg School of Management, who have forced me to develop a systematic approach to the interview process and have provided valuable insights from their work and life experiences.

Table of Contents

Preface

Most MBA job interviews offer an interesting paradox: While nearly all candidates understand the importance of taking a systematic approach to business management, few apply the same systematic approach to prepare for the interview. Instead, they approach the interview process in a haphazard manner, relying primarily on their intuition to ensure a positive outcome from the interview. This approach is, in part, based on the common belief that all interviews are company-specific and, hence, interview preparation should be done on a case-by-case basis. This is incorrect. While it is true that companies do employ diverse interviewing strategies, the core set of skills required for success is virtually the same across companies. Identifying these core skills provides candidates with a deeper understanding of recruiters' needs and enables them to develop a successful value proposition for each individual company. The goal of this book, therefore, is to outline the logic of the interview process and offer a systematic approach to acing each individual interview.

Mastering the Job Interview: The MBA Guide to the Successful Business Interview delivers a comprehensive overview of the key issues in MBA recruiting and offers in-depth insights on how to develop a winning interview strategy. This book consists of two parts. The first part introduces the basic interview principles, reveals the core skill set that most recruiters are looking for, and identifies strategies that you can use to master the job interview. This part also offers an overview of the two key components of the interview process: the personal experience interview and case analysis. The second part of this book offers an extended set of illustrations and applications identifying specific strategies on how to ace the interview process. In particular, it includes explicit interview and résumé guidelines, sample questions and answers, and strategies for the personal experience interview and case analysis.

This book is clear, concise, and to the point. It does not give you endless lists of interview questions. Instead, it walks you through the recruiting process, reveals the logic of the interview, and gives you the tools to develop your own winning interview strategy. This book is an efficient and effective learning tool that will help you master the interview and secure your most preferred job.

Good luck!

Part I: Mastering the Interview

1. The Big Picture

Companies seek to hire candidates who can add value to their organization. The interviewer's goal is to identify candidates whose value proposition best fits the needs of the organization and who have the highest potential to create value for the company. In this context, your success in the interview is determined by the degree to which your value proportion fits the company's needs.

A useful approach to maximize your fit with the company involves the following three steps: First, understand the recruiter's needs; next position yourself in a way that demonstrates you will add value to the company and differentiates you from the other candidates; finally, clearly communicate your value proposition. These three aspects of the interview process are depicted in Figure 1 and are discussed in more detail in the following sections.

Figure 1. The Interview as a Value-Delivery Process

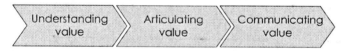

1.1. Understanding Recruiters' Needs

Recruiters are looking for candidates with skills that match the company's 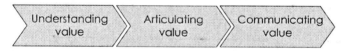 needs. The goal of the interview is to ensure a fit between a candidate's relevant competencies and a company's needs. Because most of the newly hired associates are likely to work on multiple projects and be faced with a diverse set of problems, recruiters tend to seek candidates with a broad set of skills such as leadership, analytical thinking, and teamwork – skills that can be applied across specific problems and industries. Therefore, when evaluating prospective candidates, companies tend to focus on candidates' general skills and competencies rather than on their experience related to a specific industry (e.g., pharmaceuticals, automotive, or technology). Even though industry experience is clearly beneficial, it is often viewed as a complementary asset to a candidate's core skills and competencies.

What skills are most companies looking for? An in-depth analysis of companies' recruiting practices reveals

Key attributes sought by companies

Core skills   Knowledge   Company fit

that most management consulting, consumer products, and technology companies seek future management-track associates with more or less the same set of core attributes. These attributes can be classified into three categories: (1) core skills, (2) knowledge, and (3) company fit. These three sets of core attributes are discussed in more detail in the following sections.

1.1.1. Core Skills

Core skills are the key abilities that are essential across all management functions. The core skill set includes the following eight skills:

- o *Leadership.* Leadership is the talent to take on a leadership role and is reflected in the ability to seize opportunity and take action, build a team and encourage a shared vision, keep a clear focus on the ultimate goals, and show willingness to take a personal risk to achieve these goals.

- o *Analytical skills.* Analytical skills reflect the capacity for strategic thinking, abstract reasoning, dealing with ambiguity, and an intuitive feel for numbers. Analytical skills are typically evaluated on two key dimensions: logical reasoning and quantitative skills.

- o *Creativity.* In an interview context, creativity refers to the ability to come up with an original approach that offers a simple solution to a complex problem.

- o *Teamwork.* Teamwork skills reflect the ability to collaborate with other teammates, both within and across functions (e.g., within marketing and with finance, operations, and accounting).

- o *Communication skills.* Communication skills reflect the ability to express ideas clearly, accurately, and succinctly, to disseminate information effectively. Communication skills include the following abilities: listening, public speaking, writing, discussing, negotiating, selling, and networking.

o **Management skills.** Management skills reflect a candidate's professional poise, as well as the ability to meet deadlines, manage multiple tasks, coordinate different projects, and perform under pressure.

o **Capacity to learn.** Capacity to learn reflects the ability to improve one's performance and acquire new skills.

o **Drive.** Drive refers to personal motivation for achievement, energy level, and perseverance. It reflects the willingness to overcome barriers, failure, and criticism, to go outside the comfort zone in order to achieve the set goals.

Companies vary in the degree to which they value the relative importance of the above skills. Some companies place emphasis on a subset of these skills and seek candidates who excel only on some of these dimensions (provided, of course, that they have no deficiencies on the other dimensions). In addition, different companies use different labels for the same underlying skill (e.g., innovation instead of creativity, collaboration instead of teamwork, and motivation instead of drive). Note, however, that even though companies differ in terms of the relative importance of the required skills, as well as in terms of the specific labels used to refer to these skills, the underlying skill set is essentially the same across all companies.

To illustrate, one of the key skills sought by Procter & Gamble in its recruiting efforts is the *ability to leverage resources*, which encompasses three key skills: leadership, innovation, and collaboration. In this context, leveraging resources translates to a candidate's ability to lead the company's innovation (creativity) efforts by collaborating (teamwork) with different stakeholders such as research teams, ad agencies, product development teams, and operation teams.

In the area of management consulting, McKinsey & Company is looking for candidates who demonstrate capabilities in four critical areas: problem solving (analytical skills + creativity), achieving (management skills + drive), personal impact (teamwork + communication skills), and leadership. Rather than focusing on one particular skill, McKinsey seeks well-rounded individuals with outstanding potential in each of these areas. Additional examples of company-specific core skills are offered in Appendix A.

1.1.2. Knowledge

Recruiters are also often interested in the candidate's knowledge in specific areas of interest to the interviewing company. The types of knowledge most recruiters are looking for in a candidate can be organized into three general categories: functional knowledge, industry knowledge, and global knowledge.

o *Functional knowledge* reflects the candidate's familiarity with the particular functional area (e.g., marketing, accounting, finance, and consulting). Functional knowledge involves understanding the basic business terminology, principles, frameworks, and theories that are essential for performing a given business function (see Appendix I for examples).

o *Industry knowledge* refers to the candidate's familiarity with the specifics of the industry that is of interest to the recruiting company. Industry knowledge involves understanding the industry trends, the core competencies and strategic assets of the key players, as well as the dynamics of the competition and power structure.

o *Global knowledge* refers to the candidate's familiarity with the specifics of doing business in a particular country and/or geographic area. Global knowledge involves language skills, familiarity with a country-specific culture, politics, and legal system, and, on rare occasions, even connections with local government officials, business leaders, and celebrities.

1.1.3. Company Fit

In addition to the basic functional skills, recruiters look for certain individual characteristics that will ensure a better fit between the company and the candidate. Factors that are likely to ensure the candidate's fit with the company can be organized into three general categories: personality fit, commitment to the company, and interest in the functional area.

o *Personality fit.* Personality fit reflects various aspects of a candidate's personality in relation to the company's culture (e.g., Would the candidate be able to adapt easily to the company culture? Is the candidate fun to work with?).

o **Commitment to the company.** This factor reflects the degree to which the candidate is really interested in the company. Needless to say, recruiters prefer candidates who have a sincere interest in their company.

o **Interest in the functional area.** This factor refers to the candidate's interest in the particular functional area involved (marketing, consulting, general management, research, etc.) The underlying assumption is that the greater the fit between a candidate's interests and the job requirements, the greater the likelihood that this candidate will make a valuable contribution to the company.

1.2. Articulating Your Value Proposition

Once recruiters' needs have been identified, the next step is to articulate your value proposition vis-à-vis these needs. The goal is to identify a corresponding skill that you can bring to the company for each of the key skills sought by recruiters. A four-step approach to articulating your value proposition is shown in Figure 2 and discussed in more detail below.

Figure 2. Articulating Your Value Proposition

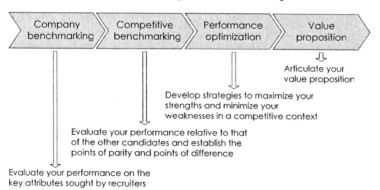

The first step is to evaluate your performance on the key attributes sought by recruiters (a.k.a. company benchmarking). One simple strategy to accomplish this is to rank your performance on each attribute on a five-point scale (e.g., exceptional, above average, average, below average, poor). This will help identify areas in which you fit the company's needs, as well as areas in which you have to improve. In general, you should strive to improve in areas in which your performance is below average (or poor), as well as in areas highly valued by the company in which your performance is merely average.

The next step is to benchmark your performance relative to that of other candidates and establish the points of parity and points of difference (a.k.a. competitive benchmarking). Because you will be compared to other candidates, it is not sufficient to be just *good*: You have to be *better* than the other candidates. One simple benchmarking method is to identify areas in which you are readily differentiated from other candidates (points of differences) and areas in which you are likely to blend in (points of parity). You can use the same five-point scale (e.g., exceptional, above average, average, below average, poor) as in the first step, but in this case your reference point is the performance of the other candidates rather than the needs of the company.

The next step is to develop strategies to maximize your strengths and minimize your weaknesses in a competitive context (a.k.a. performance optimization). This is an important step often overlooked by candidates and career counselors alike. Beware of hiding your weaknesses during the interview; this is only a temporary solution that might eventually backfire if you are not able to perform up to the standards of the company. The goal here is to improve your performance on the key attributes sought by recruiters, as well as to convert points of parity on the key attributes into points of difference. To illustrate, if you are aware that a given company emphasizes teamwork and your performance on that attribute is similar to that of the other candidates, you should consider working to improve your teamwork skills to develop a distinct advantage.

The final step is to articulate your value proposition and develop a positioning strategy. Positioning is derived by highlighting one or two aspects of your overall value proposition that most clearly communicate your value to the company and differentiate you from the other candidates. Therefore, successful positioning requires you to clearly demonstrate that your value proposition offers a better fit with the company's needs than that of the other candidates. A summary of the process of articulating your value proposition is given in the worksheet shown in Table 1.

Table 1: Value Articulation Worksheet

Value Proposition	Importance to the company ['=low, 5=high]	Your performance ['=low, 5=high]	Your relative performance ['=low, 5=high]
Core skills			
Leadership			
Analytical skills			
Creativity			
Teamwork			
Communication skills			
Management skills			
Capacity to learn			
Drive			
Knowledge			
Functional knowledge			
Industry knowledge			
Global knowledge			
Company fit			
Personality fit			
Commitment to the company			
Interest in the functional area			

Your unique value proposition:

1.3. Communicating Your Value Proposition

Once you understand the key value drivers for the company and articulate your unique value proposition, the next step is to communicate your value proposition to the recruiting company. Communicating your value proposition to the company starts with your résumé. Your résumé will not only get you the interview but will also anchor the interview discussion. The actual interview consists of several parts. It starts with an introduction, followed by questions about your personal experience and often by a case analysis. Most interviewers also give candidates an opportunity to ask questions about the company. The interview usually concludes with a closure in which the candidate highlights his/her value to the interviewing company and establishes a follow-up procedure (Figure 3). Each of these interview components is discussed in more detail below.

Figure 3. Communicating Your Value Proposition

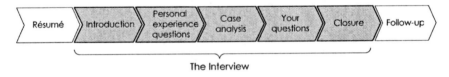

The Interview

1.3.1. Your Résumé

The basic idea is very simple: The "perfect" résumé is the one that most clearly communicates your unique value proposition to the interviewing company. Therefore, your résumé should be unique and differentiate you from the other candidates; it should underscore your value proposition and reflect your unique experience. Do not try to emulate someone else's résumé; instead, try to communicate your own story and your own value proposition.

Contrary to popular belief, your résumé is not about what you have done in the past. It is about what you can do for the company in the future. Therefore, each statement on your résumé should serve the purpose of communicating to the interviewer your value proposition and thus moving a step closer to eliciting an offer. As a general rule, avoid including in your résumé facts and/or details that do not enhance your overall value to the company. For each experience on your résumé, have a short example that demonstrates the skills important to the interviewing company (see the storyboard approach and the skills-in-context matrix in the following sections). An overview of the key résumé-writing principles is given in Appendix B.

1.3.2. Introduction

Most interviews begin with an introduction in which the interviewer and the candidate greet one another and exchange a few ice-breaking comments. It is also common for the interviewer to offer a beverage (water, coffee, tea, soda). The interview is then commonly initiated with an open-ended general question of the "tell-me-about-yourself" type – a question that also serves as the transition to the personal experience portion of the interview. Because the tell-me-about-yourself question is a quite common interview approach, it is important to master a few introductory phrases so you can readily start the interview by positioning yourself in a way that is likely to maximize your value to the company and differentiate you from the other candidates.

1.3.3. Personal Experience Interview

The personal experience interview (also referred to as a behavioral interview) aims to reveal candidates' core skills, knowledge, and their fit with the company. This part of the interview usually involves asking the candidate to provide examples of a situation in which he/she has demonstrated the set of skills that are important to the recruiting company. The nature of the personal experience interview and strategies for mastering it are discussed in more detail in Chapter 2 of this book.

1.3.4. Case Analysis

Case analysis is an integral part of many consulting, management, and marketing interviews. Case questions ask candidates to analyze a business problem with the interviewer, whereby a candidate's insights into the case are used to help evaluate the candidate's skills, knowledge, and fit with the company. A more detailed discussion of case analysis is offered in Chapter 3 of this book.

1.3.5. Your Questions

Many recruiters also let candidates ask questions about both the company and the job. Before you ask a question, think about what is important to you about the particular job and then formulate your key questions in advance. Be prepared to ask questions about the company, its vision, defining characteristics, working environment, the role that newly hired associates are likely to play, and their likely career track. Do not ask generic questions and questions that could easily be found in company literature. Instead, ask questions that will help you determine if you are a good match for the position and vice versa. Keep in mind that your questions about the company are also part of the interview. The questions you ask indicate what is really important to you and are often used to evaluate your fit with the company's goals and value system.

1.3.6. Closure

Closing the interview gives you the option to summarize your unique value proposition and reiterate your interest in the company. You can also ask whether you can provide the interviewer with any additional information and gather more information about the next step in the process (e.g., the hiring decision process and timeframe). In addition, you can inquire about how to contact the interviewer to follow up on the interview (e.g., by mail, email, or phone). Keep in mind that there are many ways to close the interview; your closing should fit your personality and the interviewing style of the recruiting company.

1.3.7. Follow-up

Many recruiters view the post-interview follow-up as an important part of the process. As a result, even though a follow-up activity does not guarantee that you will secure the position, if done well it could enhance your chances. In general, the goal of the follow-up is threefold: (1) thank the interviewer for his/her time and the opportunity to interview for the position, (2) reiterate your interest in the company and the position, and (3) reinforce your unique value proposition to the company. In this context, the follow-up can be an important component of communicating your value proposition to the company.

A common practice is to follow up the interview within 24 hours, either with a thank-you letter, email, or telephone call. The course and the outcome of the interview should help you determine the best follow-up strategy, the content of your message, and the method of communicating it.

1.3.8. Presentation

Presentation is an important and often overlooked part of the interview. Your attire and body language are two key factors that play an important role in evaluating your fit with the company. These factors are briefly discussed below.

Attire. Your attire should fit the image of the company with which you are interviewing. The more formal and/or conservative the company, the more formally and conservatively you should dress, and vice versa. If in doubt, err on the side of being more formal/conservative. The key is to be yourself and feel comfortable in your outfit (if you cannot feel comfortable in an outfit that fits the company's image, you should not interview with that company to begin with).

Body language. There are many different theories about how to interpret body language. Crossed arms (considered to be defensive); tapping your feet, playing with your hair, fidgeting (an indication of nervousness or boredom); and lack of eye contact are commonly viewed as negative signs. In contrast, leaning forward and nodding while listening are usually viewed as positive signs. Keep in mind, however, that it is all very subjective. Because most recruiters are fairly experienced in seeing through candidates' attempts to pretend to be something they are not, the best strategy is to try to be "natural." This is easier said than done; it requires a lot of practice to feel comfortable in an interview. The best approach for controlling body language is to practice, watch a recording of yourself, and/or collect feedback during mock interviews.

A set of specific interview suggestions and guidelines on how to best communicate your value proposition is given in Appendix C.

2. The Personal Experience Interview

2.1. Overview

The personal experience part of the interview (also referred to as the "behavioral" or "informational" interview) is about getting to know the candidate. There is no fixed format or agenda. This part of the interview usually involves asking the candidate to provide an example of a situation in which he/she has demonstrated a particular skill (e.g., leadership, analytical, etc.). These questions often begin with "tell me about a time when ..." or "give me an example of ...." The goal is to let the candidates demonstrate their mastery of the key skills by recounting a relevant story from their past experience. An illustration of different questions typically given in the personal experience interview is given in Appendixes C and D.

A frequent mistake made by candidates is using general skill descriptors such as "analytic," "creative," and "leadership skills." It is not uncommon to hear a candidate claiming to be "a natural leader and team player, with analytic and problem-solving skills." As a result, interviewers are likely to hear the same answers repeatedly. This is because most candidates use the same strategy to prepare for interviews: They identify their competencies and attributes, research the industry, company, and job description, and rehearse guidebook answers to typical questions. Therefore, it is important that a candidate thinks from the point of the interviewer, who is faced with a number of candidates, all claiming to have leadership, analytical, and communication skills, to be team players, and to provide the perfect fit for the interviewer's company.

The problem with simply labeling yourself as "analytic," "creative," and "strategic" is twofold. First, these are very general concepts and, as such, they lack specific meaning. A candidate who states that he/she "has analytical skills" does not communicate any relevant information to the interviewer (except that he/she has figured out that being "analytic" is important). The interviewer cannot even be sure that the candidate actually understands what being "analytic" means. What the interviewer is looking for is a story that reveals the candidate's particular skill.

The second issue in using general skill descriptors such as "analytic," "creative," and "strategic" is that recruiting is not just a process of evaluating each candidate but is a *choice* among candidates. Your goal is not only to convince the interviewer that you fit the position requirements but also that you are the *best* among all candidates. Hence, you need to differentiate yourself. Simply saying that you are "analytic," "creative," and a "team player" will not differentiate you, because a great number of other candidates will be rehearsing exactly the same phrases and claiming the same attributes.

A successful interview communicates your value proposition in a meaningful and memorable way that will establish your superiority to the other candidates. This can best be achieved by describing specific instances that vividly demonstrate your particular skills. Tell your story, not a textbook example. Your story should be specific and demonstrate your skills in a particular context. Make your story colorful and expressive, which will make it stand out and be more memorable. A vivid story has a greater chance to make the interviewer relate to your experience, pay attention, and become more involved in the interview. The story you tell presents an opportunity to create a positive and lasting impression that will allow the interviewer to later link your story to your name and image.

Think of the interview as an opportunity to communicate your value proposition while differentiating yourself from other candidates. Think of it as a marketing communication task in which you must convince the interviewer that you can satisfy his/her company's needs better than the other candidates. You do not see many ads in which a company simply claims product superiority. Instead, a good ad tells you a story that demonstrates the product's benefits in a specific context. You should do the same. The storyboard approach discussed in the following section shows you how to achieve that.

2.2. The Introduction Question

The interview typically starts with an introduction question asking candidates to offer an overview of who they are, of their career achievements, and/or their life so far. The prototypical introduction question is "Tell me about yourself." This question is so common that not having a ready answer is inexcusable. Yet, many candidates come to interviews without a prepared answer and instead try to make up an answer on the spot. Even among those who do have a ready answer, many give a textbook cliché introduction, thus failing to take advantage of the opportunity afforded by this question to articulate their value proposition and differentiate themselves from the other candidates. Therefore, it is crucial not only to have a ready introduction, but also to have an introduction that will give you an edge over the other candidates and will bring you closer to receiving an offer.

A useful approach to developing a meaningful introduction is to structure your answer around four key elements: overview, accomplishments, skills, and value. These four elements, illustrated in Figure 4, can be summarized as follows:

 o The *overview* is a brief introduction statement summarizing your most important and/or most distinct characteristics.

 o The overview is then followed by a summary of your key *accomplishments* that should give the interviewer a better picture of what you have achieved so far in your professional career.

 o Building on your accomplishments, highlight the key *skills* and competencies you have accumulated so far.

o Finally, articulate your *value* to the recruiter's company by offering a summary of how/why you, with your skills and accomplishments, are positioned to create value for the company better than any of the other candidates.

Figure 4. Structuring the Answer to the Introduction Question

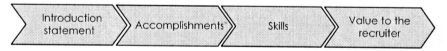

When preparing for the introduction question, keep in mind that your answer not only gives you the option to articulate your value proposition to the company early on in the interview; it also gives you the option to change the course of the interview by focusing the interviewer's attention on the accomplishments, skills, and value highlighted in your answer. Indeed, it is often the case that issues brought up by candidates in the introduction become the focal points of the interview.

It is also important to keep in mind that in most cases you will not be able to control the pace of the interview; instead you will have to follow the pace set by the interviewer. This implies that you should have several versions of your introduction: a brief version and a few extended ones. However, given that this is an introduction, even the most detailed version of your answer still needs to be short and to the point.

2.3. The Storyboard Approach

The storyboard approach introduced here is based on the relatively simple idea of telling vivid and detailed stories to communicate your skills in a specific context. Instead of simply claiming that you have "analytical skills," tell a story that demonstrates how you applied these skills to solve a specific problem. Not only is this more likely to convince the interviewer that you actually have the skill, it will also make you more distinct and your story more memorable.

To make your story engaging, informative, and impactful, you can use the following three-step format, illustrated in Figure 5:

o   Start by describing the decision *context*. Describe the decision environment and the problem that you were trying to solve.

o   Then describe how you approached the problem and what *actions* you took. Be specific and identify how you were able to solve the problem, what your strategy was, and how you carried out this strategy. Make sure to underscore how you personally made a difference.

o   Finally, describe the *results*. Quantify the outcome, if possible, and be sure to explain what qualifies that outcome as a success.

Figure 5. Personal Experience Interview: The Storyboard Approach

The key element in the context-action-results (C-A-R) approach is the action step, which often is the focal point of the story. A useful format for presenting a problem-driven action involves the

following approach. Start by summarizing what you did to solve the problem and then, time permitting, elaborate on the specific steps describing your action. These include: (1) identifying the problem, (2) generating several possible solution scenarios, (3) gathering additional information, (4) soliciting input from others, (5) selecting the best alternative, (6) designing a plan to implement the proposed solution in a timely manner, and (7) evaluating the results to learn from the experience. Common techniques for communicating your accomplishments are shown in Appendix H.

In addition to the context-action-results model, another conceptually similar approach is the **situation-task-action-results**, or S-T-A-R model. Here situation refers to the problem at hand and task refers to your assignment – what you were asked to do or, in cases where you initiated the action, how you interpreted the situation and formulated the task. As can be seen from Figure 6, both C-A-R and S-T-A-R approaches are essentially identical. Some prefer the C-A-R approach because it is simple and more intuitive. Others prefer to use the S-T-A-R approach because it sounds more relevant to a candidate's situation: Everyone wants to be a "star" in the job market. Ultimately, the choice between the C-A-R and the S-T-A-R approach is arbitrary – use whichever one you feel more comfortable with.

Figure 6. The Storyboard Approach: C-A-R and S-T-A-R Frameworks

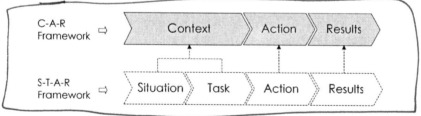

2.4. The Skills-in-Context Matrix

The storyboard approach is very useful for illustrating a specific skill (e.g., leadership) in a particular context (e.g., prior job). There are, however, multiple skills that are of interest to interviewers. There are also multiple contexts in which these skills can be shown: prior work experience, prior academic experience, various extracurricular activities, etc. Therefore, it is important to have a system for navigating through different skills in different contexts during the interview. This system is the skills-in-context matrix.

The skills-in-context matrix cross-tabulates the key skills and the different contexts in which these skills can be demonstrated. An illustration of the skills-in-context matrix is shown in Figure 7. The skills factor of the matrix comprises the eight key skills identified in the previous section: leadership, analytical skills, creativity, teamwork, communication skills, management skills, capacity to learn, and drive. The context factor, on the other hand, is represented by the different experiences that provide an environment in which some or all of the above skills might be exhibited.

Figure 7. The Skills-in-Context Matrix

	Context 1	Context 2	Context 3	Context 4
Leadership	C-A-R	C-A-R	C-A-R	C-A-R
Analytical skills	C-A-R	C-A-R	C-A-R	C-A-R
Creativity	C-A-R	C-A-R	C-A-R	C-A-R
Teamwork	C-A-R	C-A-R	C-A-R	C-A-R
Communication skills	C-A-R	C-A-R	C-A-R	C-A-R
Management skills	C-A-R	C-A-R	C-A-R	C-A-R
Capacity to learn	C-A-R	C-A-R	C-A-R	C-A-R
Drive	C-A-R	C-A-R	C-A-R	C-A-R

For MBA students, the usual contexts are their college experience, prior job experience(s), MBA program experience (team projects, club involvement, etc.), as well as various extracurricular activities (sports, volunteer work, hobbies, etc.). Some of the contexts, such as prior job experience and academic experience, are typical for all candidates. Others are more specific, and it is up to the candidate to introduce that context during the interview (either in the conversation or by featuring it in the résumé).

A common mistake made by candidates is their lack of a systematic approach to linking specific skills to specific contexts (e.g., analytic skills in college, leadership in prior job, teamwork during the MBA program). As a result, candidates are often unprepared to address interviewers' questions about a specific skill in a particular context (e.g., "tell me about your leadership skills at your most recent job"). To correct that, the skills-in-context approach calls for a story that demonstrates each of the key skills in each of the contexts implied by the candidate's background. Thus, when asked about a specific skill (e.g., leadership), you will be prepared to tell a story demonstrating this skill across different contexts (skill-based stories). When asked about a specific context (e.g., prior work experience) you have readily available stories that demonstrate your relevant skill set (context-based stories). You also will have a ready story when asked to discuss a specific skill (e.g., leadership) in a particular context (e.g., prior job).

To illustrate, consider a candidate who held two jobs prior to enrolling in an MBA program. The natural contexts in which this candidate's skills could have been demonstrated are (1) college experience, (2) job #1, (3) job #2, and (4) current MBA experience. To be prepared for the interview, this candidate should be ready to discuss each of the eight key skills in each of the above four contexts (Figure 8). If, for example, this candidate is asked to talk about his/her leadership skills at job #2, he/she should have a ready story that describes the company context, the action taken, and the results.

The skills-in-context approach requires a substantial amount of thinking on a candidate's part. In many cases it is difficult to come up with examples of different skills in all contexts. Yet, articulating specific instances that demonstrate each relevant skill in different contexts can go a long way to ensure that the candidate has effectively communicated his/her value proposition to the interviewer.

Figure 8. Skills-in-Context Matrix: An Example

	College	Job #1	Job #2	MBA
Leadership	C-A-R	C-A-R	**C-A-R**	C-A-R
Analytical skills	C-A-R	C-A-R	C-A-R	C-A-R
Creativity	C-A-R	C-A-R	C-A-R	C-A-R
Teamwork	C-A-R	C-A-R	C-A-R	C-A-R
Communication skills	C-A-R	C-A-R	C-A-R	C-A-R
Management skills	C-A-R	C-A-R	C-A-R	C-A-R
Capacity to learn	C-A-R	C-A-R	C-A-R	C-A-R
Drive	C-A-R	C-A-R	C-A-R	C-A-R

Leadership at Job #2:

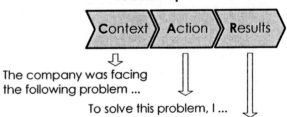

Context ⟩ Action ⟩ Results

The company was facing the following problem ...

To solve this problem, I ...

As a result, the company's revenues increased by 15% ...

3. Case Analysis

Being a successful manager requires the ability to deal creatively with complex problems and to reach logical conclusions based on the available facts in a short timeframe. Because no particular background or set of qualifications prepares candidates for that, many companies have come to rely on the case analysis approach as an integral part of the interview process.

Case interviews test a candidate's ability to solve problems on the spot. Case analysis not only allows interviewers to examine a candidate's ability to think logically and articulate an answer, it also allows them to observe a candidate's thought processes, tolerance for ambiguity and data overload, poise, self-confidence, and communication skills under pressure. For that reason, case analysis is an important part of the interview. It demonstrates a candidate's ability to navigate the issues in search of the most logical solution. As an additional benefit, the interactive nature of the case interview adds a dynamic dimension to understanding a candidate's personality and allows better evaluation of the fit between the candidate and the interviewer's company.

Case analysis involves two types of problems: business cases and brainteasers. Business cases deal with business problems such as profitability, market share, mergers and acquisitions, new product launch decisions, etc. Brainteasers, in contrast, deal with logical problems across different contexts. These two types of cases are discussed in more detail in the following sections.

```
        Case analysis
       ┌───────┴───────┐
    Business      Brainteaser
    cases           cases
```

3.1. Business Cases

3.1.1. Business Case Basics

Case analysis examines a candidate's approach to a complex situation and tests skills and competencies to identify and solve complex problems. Case analysis places particular emphasis on factors that are more difficult to test in the context of the traditional interview. These factors include logical reasoning and quantitative analysis (analytical skills), creative problem solving (creativity), the ability to clearly express your point of view (communication skills), and professional poise and ability to perform under pressure (management skills).

In a case interview, the candidate is introduced to a particular business scenario and asked to analyze the situation and offer a solution. The interview proceeds as an open dialogue between the interviewer and the candidate in which the candidate's goal is to identify the source of the problem and recommend a solution.

The key issue to keep in mind is that case analysis is not about the solution per se; it is about how you arrive at that solution. Rather than looking for one specific answer, interviewers are trying to understand how you think. In this context, the interviewer is more interested in your assumptions, your selection of a framework, and the quality of your reasoning than in whether you arrive at the "right answer" (which, as a matter of fact, often does not exist).

A good strategy to approach case analysis is to think of the interview as a problem-solving task in which you work through hypothetical business problems; try to forget that this is an interview and think as of it as a consulting assignment in which the interviewer is the client. Your goal should be to solve your client's problem rather than guess at the "right" answer. Remember that the interviewer's goal is to hire a person who will be solving business problems on a day-to-day basis and, hence, needs to feel comfortable with the process. An overview of the basic case interview strategies is given in Appendix J.

3.1.2. Business Case Format

Business cases can be presented in one of two formats: oral and written. These two formats are discussed in more detail below.

Oral cases are presented in an interactive manner: they offer very little information up front and leave it up to the candidate to uncover the case specifics. Oral cases are very popular among recruiters, especially during the early rounds of interviews, because they provide excellent insights into candidates' ability to identify the relevant information, decision processes, and interpersonal skills. Common types of business cases include advising a client about an acquisition, responding to a competitive move by another company in the industry, and evaluating opportunities for a new product introduction. Business problems are often phrased as "CEO questions" or "client questions." For example: "You are the

CEO of a telecommunications company and your profits are falling despite the overall category growth. What do you do?" or "You have been hired to advise a major consumer goods company that is considering launching a new line of lunch cereals. How would you advise your client?"

In addition to the typical business problems, interviews can involve behavioral cases that deal with relationship-building and team-management issues. A common behavioral case involves a client project in which something has gone wrong, and the goal is to resolve the problem, control the damage, and deal with the team and/or the client. The candidate might be asked to explain what he/she will do to resolve the situation or, alternatively, he/she might be asked to role play the interaction.

Written cases are usually several pages long and are accompanied by data exhibits that contain supplemental information. Candidates usually are given time to read the case and prepare for a discussion. Written cases offer insights into a candidate's ability for logical reasoning and quantitative skills, as well as the ability to interpret complex data patterns. An important part of written case analysis involves interpreting different data patterns, usually presented in the form of a chart and/or a table. The goal is to assess candidates' ability to interpret data presented in different formats and their ability to derive conclusions from these data. This type of case is often used by recruiters during advanced rounds of the interview, although some consulting companies (e.g., Bain & Company) tend to use written cases during the early rounds as well.

Written cases can also be tested in both an individual and group context. In a group case analysis, each of the candidates is given a written case and a set of specific questions to be answered. After reading the case, candidates take part in a group discussion in which they present their solution and comment on the solutions presented by other team members. Recruiters are looking for candidates who can present their own findings, integrate the input from other team members, and comment on the solutions presented by other team members. In this context, group interviews are a litmus test for a candidate's leadership abilities, interpersonal skills, and collaborative spirit.

3.1.3. How to Approach the Case

The case interview typically starts with a brief description of a business scenario such as a client facing declining market share, eroding profit margins, or a new product introduction. Recruiters are not looking for candidates who happen to know the right answer and "crack the case," but rather for people who have a system that will allow them to solve *any* case. Indeed, even though each problem requires its own unique analysis, most companies believe that the process of analyzing various business problems has a common structure that carries across different scenarios. Therefore, when discussing the case, it is important to apply a logical, well-structured approach that enables you to reach a meaningful conclusion.

A common approach to case analysis includes four steps: clarify, structure, analyze, and conclude. These four steps to case analysis are logically connected (Figure 9). First, determine the situation, identify the problem, and verify the facts; next, develop and present a framework for analyzing the problem; then, apply the framework to analyze specific problems and derive effective solutions; finally, make a recommendation. These steps are outlined in more detail below.

Figure 9. Structuring the Case Interview

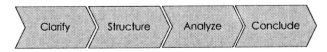

Clarify. The first step is to make sure that you understand the business scenario and the question you are being asked. In fact, one of the most common mistakes during a case interview is misunderstanding the question or answering the wrong question. Sometimes the interviewer will deliberately interject ambiguity into the problem as a part of the interview. Ask clarification questions if you are unclear about certain aspects of the case. A simple strategy to start case analysis is to paraphrase the question to ensure that you understand the problem.

Structure. Structuring involves choosing an approach (framework) to solve the problem. It is a good idea to describe your overall approach and explain the logic used to address the problem. Try to find the appropriate framework to break the problem into separate issues, but do not force-fit a framework to the problem. Remember that your goal is not to showcase your knowledge of a particular framework but to demonstrate your ability to solve business problems. Frameworks are tools to help you organize your thinking; they are not the solution to the problem. It is a good idea to explain the reasons for selecting the framework you use and how you would go about applying the framework to the problem at hand. When given a complex problem, think broadly and be sure to cover all relevant issues rather than spending all your time on one particular issue (unless the interviewer asks you to do so).

Analyze. There are three basic components to a solid analysis: facts, assumptions, and logic.

o *Facts* are the cornerstones of your analysis and are used to derive your assumptions, logical conclusions, and proposed actions. Some of the facts might not be readily available, and you will have to ask the interviewer to fill in the gaps. As a general rule, the shorter the case, the greater the likelihood that you will have to request additional information as you analyze the problem.

o *Assumptions* are necessary to fill in the missing facts. Making assumptions is a common practice in business analysis; the key is to ensure that your assumptions are realistic and clearly articulated. Use sensitivity analysis (e.g., compare an aggressive vs. a conservative scenario) when unsure about the validity of a particular assumption (e.g., market share growth, rate of new product adoption).

o *Logic* links the available information (facts and assumptions) to uncover new relationships (e.g., cause-and-effect), derive conclusions (e.g., if ... then...), and/or apply general business principles to the case at hand (e.g., an increase in price is likely to lead to a decrease in quantity sold). Break the problem into separate issues, address the issues one at a time, and state findings for each analysis. Remember that the interview is not about the outcome (i.e., getting the "right" answer) but about the process of getting the problem solved. Walk the interviewer through your thinking, and use visual aids (flowchart, matrix, bullet points) when possible.

Conclude. Conclude the case discussion by summarizing your logic and offering a recommendation that reflects your decision on how the company should address the situation described in the case. The proposed solution should be clear and based on your

27

evaluation of facts, assumptions, and logic, rather than on unsubstantiated opinions. Link your recommendation back to the problem and identify how your solution will solve the problem. A useful format to keep in mind is problem ⇨ solution ⇨ justification: Briefly identify the problem, outline the proposed solution, and explain its rationale.

A set of specific case interview suggestions and winning strategies is given in Appendix J.

3.1.4. Common Business Problems

Depending on the nature of the underlying problem, most business cases can be classified into two categories: action-based and problem-based. These two case types are discussed in more detail below.

Action-based cases deal with scenarios in which the company is considering a specific strategic action such as launching a new product (and/or choosing between two new product ideas), repositioning an existing product/service/brand, entering new markets, acquiring or merging with another company. Your goal is to evaluate the viability of the proposed action; that is, whether or not the company should go ahead. To illustrate: "Your client has to decide whether or not to acquire a sports drink company. You have been asked to assess the long-term attractiveness of the sports drink market and advise your client on the viability of his acquisition strategy." Company actions might also be related to the tactical implementation of an offering and involve optimizing the performance of specific tactical attributes such as product, service, brand, price, promotions, and distribution. To illustrate: "How would you set the price for product X?" or "You are a CEO of a large financial services company and have decided to launch a new service for your customers. How would you promote this service?"

Problem-based cases involve optimizing the performance of an existing business program rather than developing a new program. Problem-based cases are defined by the presence of a *performance gap*: a discrepancy between the desired and the actual state of affairs, between the goal and the reality. To illustrate, a decrease in a company's profitability (the problem) can be viewed as a strategic gap between the company's desire to grow profitability (goal) and the decrease in market share (reality). Other examples of performance gaps include discrepancies between desired and actual profit margins, revenues, and market share. To illustrate, common performance gap problems are: "We have trouble achieving our profitability (or market share) targets," "Our business is not growing fast enough," "Our sales are dropping," or "Our market share is declining, despite the overall growth of the category." In this context, the goal of case analysis is to solve the problem by identifying its source and suggesting a viable strategy to close the performance gap.

In addition to cases that deal with performance gaps, another type of problem-based cases deals with evaluating a change in the environment. These cases depict scenarios that involve a significant change in the environment in which the company operates. Such changes might include a new competitive entry, a competitive (re)action (e.g., new product introduction, price change, aggressive promotions, superiority claim), changes in customer demand, changes in technology, legal regulations, and government policies. For example, typical change-in-the-environment problems are: "Our company is facing new competitors" and "Our customers are becoming more concerned with a healthy lifestyle." An illustration of different action-based and problem-based case questions is given in Appendix K.

3.1.5. Using Frameworks in Case Analysis

Employing a framework for solving business problems is vital for successful case analysis. Recruiting companies are not particularly interested in the candidate's solution to the problem at hand; instead, they are interested in this candidate's ability to apply a systematic approach to solving diverse business problems. Yet, the selection and use of frameworks are among the most common mistakes candidates make. Because of its complexity, the issue of using frameworks in case analysis is addressed in a separate book: *Mastering the Case Analysis: The MBA Guide to Management, Marketing, and Strategic Consulting Case Interviews.*

3.2. Brainteaser Cases

Brainteaser questions seek to directly test a candidate's creative problem-solving and logical reasoning skills. While not all interviewers use brainteasers, they are very common among management consulting and software companies. Unlike traditional business cases, brainteasers usually are abstract questions describing a specific (often non-business) problem. Although some questions might require certain factual knowledge, most brainteasers are self-contained logical tasks. There are three main types of brainteasers: (1) estimation cases (e.g., How many piano tuners are there in the world?), (2) logical cases (e.g., Why do Coke cans have an indent on the bottom?), and (3) creative cases (e.g., How would you move Mount Fuji?). These three types of brainteasers are described in more detail in the following sections.

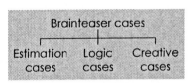

3.2.1. Estimation Cases

The popularity of estimation cases in management consulting interviews stems from the fact that these questions are not only easy to create, discuss, and evaluate, but also that they are representative of the type of problems managers and consultants face in their day-to-day work. Estimation questions typically require both logical deduction and quantitative skills. Their goal is not to test factual knowledge but, instead, to observe the candidate's approach to problem solving. In this context, the answer, per se, is often irrelevant; what counts is the process of arriving at the answer.

Estimation cases can vary from market sizing problems in which the candidate has to determine the size of a particular market (e.g., What is the size of the market for the Segway human transporter?) to estimating physical factors such as weight and volume (e.g., How much does the moon weigh?). Additional examples of estimation questions and solution strategies are given in Appendix L.

Estimating questions can sometimes be part of a more comprehensive case analysis. To illustrate, the answer to the question of whether a company should launch a new product largely depends on the size of the potential market.

While each estimation question is likely to have its unique set of solutions, two general approaches to estimation questions can be identified: analysis and analogy.

Estimation by analysis involves breaking down the object into smaller parts and estimating each part individually. For example, in the case of estimating the weight of an airplane, one might break down the problem into a series of more specific tasks such as estimating the weight of the different parts of the airplane: the body, engines, fuel, luggage, passengers, etc.

Estimation by analogy involves comparing the estimated object to a similar object with known parameters. To illustrate, when asked to estimate the number of car batteries annually sold in the United States, one can use total car sales to arrive at the answer.

Estimation cases might require certain factual knowledge to derive the final answer (e.g., the size of the U.S. population, formulas to calculate the volume/weight of an object, etc.). Knowing the facts helps, but it is not crucial. Remember, the goal of the interview is not to test whether you can get the "right" answer but to test your ability for logical reasoning. Therefore, if you do not have the necessary data readily available, describe the *process* you would use to solve the problem. In most cases describing the algorithm is more important than running the actual calculations.

3.2.2. Logic Cases

Logic cases typically describe an abstract problem based on logical reasoning. The goal is to uncover the logical principle underlying the problem. Unlike estimation and creative questions, most logical problems have a unique solution. To illustrate, consider the classic problem: How long would it take to move Mount Fuji? More examples of logic questions and solutions can be found in Appendix M.

3.2.3. Creative Cases

Creative cases are another form of brainteasers and are very popular among companies in which creativity is paramount (e.g., software, design, product development, advertising). By definition, creative cases can be about virtually anything. To illustrate, consider the following questions: How would you describe green to a blind person? How would you design a mobile phone for dogs? How would you design a restroom for a CEO? How would you develop a technology to grow straight bananas? How would you describe a pineapple to a person who has never seen one? How would you describe the business school of the future? These questions test a candidate's creativity and ability to think "outside of the box" to find an original solution to a nontrivial problem. An additional benefit of creative questions is that they lend themselves to interesting conversation that can provide further insights into the candidate's personality.

3.2.4. Preparing for a Brainteaser Interview

Because brainteaser questions lack a pre-set format, topic, and structure, one cannot really "prepare" for a brainteaser interview (which is one of the reasons that interviewers like these questions!). Practicing, however, can help you better articulate your decision process, improve your logical thinking, and help you develop your own strategy for approaching brainteaser questions.

4. The Recruiter's Decision Process

This book has identified three key performance aspects used by companies to evaluate job candidates: core skills, knowledge, and the overall fit with the company. Within each of these factors, we further identified several distinct dimensions. Leadership, analytical skills, creativity, teamwork, communication skills, management skills, capacity to learn, and drive described the core skills. Functional knowledge, industry knowledge, and global knowledge characterized different aspects of knowledge. Personality fit, commitment to the company, and interest in the functional area measured a candidate's overall fit with company. Furthermore, these fifteen dimensions are evaluated in the context of a battery of tests such as the personal experience interview; business case analysis; estimation, logic, and creative questions.

The question then is how do recruiters plan the interview process, how do they integrate a candidate's performance on each of these fifteen different dimensions into an overall evaluation, and how do they choose the most desirable candidate(s). The following discussion offers an overview of different planning and decision strategies used by interviewers.

4.1. Planning the Interview

The process of evaluating candidates' core skills, knowledge, and overall fit with the company involves several components: evaluation of a candidate's résumé; the personal experience interview; business case analysis; and estimation, logic, and creative questions.

The relative importance of these different components of the interview process varies by industry, by the functional area, and by the company. Yet, it is possible to identify common patterns of information integration across different companies. A typical example of the relative importance of different interview components on a candidate's overall evaluation is given in Table 2.

As can be seen from Table 2, the relative importance of the components varies throughout the course of the interview process. To illustrate, the résumé is a valuable tool for pre-screening candidates and forming a preliminary evaluation of their skills, knowledge, and motivation. In contrast, the personal experience interview, case analysis, and the estimation, logic, and creative questions allow specific, in-depth evaluation of different aspects of the candidate's abilities. Thus, a candidate's leadership skills are often best revealed in the personal experience interview and group business case analysis; analytical skills are typically best identified in the context of business case analysis, estimation and logical questions; creativity is best revealed in business case analysis and through the creative questions. In this context, planning the interview involves ensuring that all the relevant skills are covered by one or more of the different interview formats.

Table 2. Planning the Interview: An Example

Value Proposition	Interview Components					
	R	PEI	BC	GBC	EQ/LQ	CQ
Core skills						
Leadership	★★	★★★	★	★★★	---	---
Analytical skills	★★	★	★★★	★★★	★★★	---
Creativity	★★	★★	★★★	★★★	★★	★★★
Teamwork	★★	★★★	★★	★★★	---	---
Communication skills	★★	★★★	★★★	★★★	★★	★★
Management skills	★★	★★★	★★★	★★★	★★★	---
Capacity to learn	★★	★★	★★★	★★★	---	---
Drive	★★	★★★	★	★	---	---
Knowledge						
Functional knowledge	★★	★★	★★★	★★★	---	★★★
Industry knowledge	★★	★★★	★★	★★	---	---
Global knowledge	★★	★★★	★★	★★	---	---
Company fit						
Personality fit	★	★★★	★★	★★	---	---
Commitment to the company	---	★★★	---	---	---	---
Interest in the functional area	---	★★★	★★	★★	---	---

R = Résumé

PEI = Personal Experience Interview

BC = Business Case Analysis

GBC = Group Business Case Analysis

EQ = Estimation Questions

LQ = Logic Questions

CQ = Creative Questions

★★★ = High diagnostic value

★★ = Moderate diagnostic value

★ = Low diagnostic value

--- = Not applicable

An important component of planning the interview process is deciding on a model to be used to integrate a candidate's performance on each of the different dimensions into an overall evaluation and to choose the most desirable candidate(s). The following discussion offers an overview of different evaluation strategies used by interviewers.

4.2. Recruiters' Decision Model

From a normative viewpoint, the optimal choice strategy involves combining candidates' evaluations across different dimensions into an overall evaluation by weighting a candidate's performance on a given attribute by this attribute's importance and then choosing the candidate with the highest overall score. Analytically, this approach can be represented as follows: $E_A = w_1a_1 + w_2a_2 + ... + w_na_n$, where E_A is the overall evaluation of the candidate A, w_i is the importance of each of the attributes used to evaluate the candidate's performance, a_i is the candidate's performance on each attribute, and n is the number of attributes used to evaluate candidates.

Using the above approach requires recruiters to quantify the relative importance of the different performance attributes to the company. To illustrate, a company needs not only to decide whether the capacity to learn should be valued more, equal to, or less than industry knowledge, but also to assign a number to this relationship (e.g., capacity to learn is 1.4 times more important than industry knowledge). Because many recruiters find it difficult to quantify the relative importance of the skills sought in job candidates, they tend to use simplifying decision strategies, or heuristics, to make a choice.

One strategy to simplify the decision process is to view all performance attributes as equally important. Thus, under this assumption, factors such as capacity to learn and industry knowledge would be viewed as equally important. As a result, this simplified version of the normative approach requires recruiters to simply add up candidates' score on each of the performance attributes (i.e., $E_A = a_1 + a_2 + ... + a_n$) and then choose the one with the highest overall score (because all attribute weights w_i are equal, they are no longer a part of the evaluation formula).

Another, even simpler, evaluation strategy not only equates the relative importance of different attributes but also ignores the candidate's performance on each dimension by coding it as either acceptable or unacceptable. Thus, instead of using a rating scale, recruiters will simply use "yes" or "no" to record the candidate's performance on each relevant attribute. The candidate ultimately chosen is the one with the most "yes" marks.

An alternative strategy to simplify the evaluation process involves reducing the number of attributes used to evaluate candidates' performance. Indeed, recruiters often find it difficult to evaluate candidates on all 15 dimensions outlined in this book and, as a result, they often simplify the evaluation by either combining some of the performance dimensions or by simply ignoring attributes deemed of small importance.

In addition to making a choice by selecting the most qualified candidate, recruiters often decide using an elimination-based approach. This approach involves establishing a set of performance standards required of job candidates and eliminating all candidates that do not meet any of these standards. This approach has been prominently used in the TV show "The Apprentice," where candidates are eliminated one by one until a single candidate has been identified. In business recruiting, choosing by elimination is often used in combination with other decision rules, so that candidates who do not meet the company's desired performance profile are eliminated from the selection process, and the recruiters can focus their attention on the remaining candidates.

4.3. The Random Factor

The discussion so far has been based on the assumption that companies always manage the interview process in a systematic and logical manner. This is not always the case. Interviewing is not always a rational process, and the decisions of individual recruiters are not always guided by systematic decision models. In many cases, the hiring decision is influenced by a variety of idiosyncratic factors that are based on an interviewer's intuition about the candidate, rather than on a rational evaluation of a candidate's abilities. Reliance on intuition is reinforced by the existence of numerous interview materials offering detailed advice on how to "nail" the job interview, allowing candidates to sail trough the interview without actually having the skills sought by the company.

The logic of the interview process can also be affected by a variety of random factors particular to the situation or the specific interviewer. Simply put, this means that despite the structured nature of the interview process outlined in the earlier sections, there is a random factor that can have a significant impact on the outcome of the interview. This naturally raises the question of how a candidate can account for such unforeseeable factors. The simple answer is that controlling for such random factors is virtually impossible. Therefore, the best bet is to rely on the logic-based interview approach that is likely to work in most cases.

5. Conclusion

Your success at the job interview is determined by your ability to first identify a company that can best fulfill your goals and then convince recruiters from that company to hire you. To achieve that, you should be able to clearly articulate your value proposition to the company and identify factors that make you the best candidate for the job. Your successful interview performance is a function of your individual characteristics – your skills, knowledge, and experience – as well as your ability to optimally market these skills, knowledge, and experience to the recruiting company. Therefore, developing a systematic approach to market yourself at the interview is a necessary condition for your recruiting success.

The systematic approach to managing the job interview involves three key steps: understanding company value, articulating your unique value proposition, and, finally, communicating your value proposition to persuade the recruiter that you fit the needs of the company.

The first step, understanding company value, involves three key factors: a candidate's core skills (leadership, analytical skills, creativity, teamwork, communication skills, management skills, capacity to learn, and drive), knowledge (functional, industry, and global knowledge), and the overall fit with the company (personality fit, commitment to the company, and interest in the functional area).

The second step, articulating your value proposition, involves identifying a corresponding skill that you can bring to the company for each of the key skills sought by that company. This process involves four steps: company benchmarking (i.e., evaluating your performance on each of the attributes sought by recruiters), competitive benchmarking (i.e., evaluating your performance relative to other candidates), performance optimization (i.e., working on maximizing your relative strengths and minimizing your weaknesses), and, finally, positioning (i.e., articulating your value proposition and developing a positioning statement that highlights the most important aspects of your value to the company).

The third step, communicating your value to the company, involves presenting your value proposition in a clear, succinct, and effective manner that will convince the recruiter that you are the best candidate for the job. In this context, your résumé plays a key role, not only to get you the interview but also to anchor the personal experience questions, which are the core of the interview and are designed to test your basic skills, knowledge, and company fit. The case analysis in all of its forms (business, estimation, logic, and creativity cases) aims to test many of the key attributes that matter to recruiters in a problem-solving context. Your questions to the company are an additional indicator of your goals and values and are an important part of the interview as well. Finally, the closure and the follow-up give you the opportunity to underscore your interest in the company and reiterate the value you bring to the company.

For many candidates, recruiting is not only a process of finding a job, it is also a process of discovering who they are and/or who they want to be. Indeed, to be successful in the interview, you should not only have a good understanding of the needs of the recruiting company, you should also know yourself. Thus, recruiting is not only about the company discovering you but also about you discovering yourself: who you are and who you want to be, both personally and professionally.

Part II: References

Appendix A: Core Skills Sought by Companies

Most companies look for the same set of attributes in job candidates: core skills (leadership, analytical skills, creativity, teamwork, communication skills, management skills, capacity to learn, and drive), knowledge (functional, industry, and global knowledge), and the overall fit with the company (personality fit, commitment to the company, and interest in the functional area). And even though they look for the same skill sets in job candidates, companies vary in the way they articulate these skills. Following is a sample of the key skills sought by companies in the three most popular recruiting areas: consulting, marketing, and finance[1].

Concentration in Consulting

AT Kearney

- o Perceptive
- o Resourceful
- o Achieving
- o Teaming

Bain & Company

- o Intelligence
- o Integrity
- o Passion
- o Ambition

Booz Allen Hamilton

- o Critical thinking and problem solving
- o Creativity and insight
- o Quantitative analytics
- o Conceptual analytics
- o Business leadership
- o Personal leadership

- o Interpersonal skills
- o Intellect, knowledge, and insight
- o Interest

DiamondCluster International

- o Strong analytical and problem solving skills
- o Ability to add value and influence change
- o Ability to work effectively in a team environment
- o Demonstrated initiative and leadership
- o Strong written and verbal communication skills
- o Creativity and resourcefulness
- o Honesty and integrity
- o Commitment and reliability
- o Adaptability and flexibility

Grant Thornton

- o Hard working
- o Creative
- o Passion for excellence
- o Integrity
- o Teamwork

Kurt Salmon Associates

- o Integrity
- o Drive to excel
- o Strong analytical and communication skills
- o Personal resilience
- o Team players
- o Commitment

L.E.K. Consulting

- o Intelligence
- o Honesty
- o Hard work
- o Integrity
- o Teamwork
- o Good humor

Marakon Associates

- o Structured and logical thinking
- o A creative and analytical approach to problem solving
- o Empathy, maturity, and professionalism
- o An understanding of the business issues confronting CEOs and general management
- o Ability to work and communicate effectively with clients and colleagues at all levels
- o Desire to achieve high standards both personally and professionally
- o Common sense

Mars & Company

- o Strong quantitative skills
- o Energy
- o Maturity
- o Creativity
- o Uncommon common sense
- o A sense of humor

McKinsey & Company

- o Problem solving
- o Achieving
- o Personal impact
- o Leadership

Mercer Management Consulting

- o The ability to structure problems logically
- o The ability to develop innovative yet practical solutions
- o The ability to work effectively as members of a team
- o The ability to communicate clearly with both colleagues and clients
- o The ability to take initiative and leadership both internally and with clients

Monitor Group

- o Capabilities
- o Capacity to learn
- o Commitment

ZS Associates

- o Analytical and quantitative skills
- o Strategic thinking
- o Personal presence
- o Business acumen
- o Strong communication skills
- o Commitment
- o Collegiality
- o Creativity

Concentration in Marketing

American Express

- o Ability to develop winning strategies and drive results
- o Strong focus on customer and client service
- o Personal excellence
- o Ability to drive innovation and change
- o Ability to build important relationships
- o Ability to communicate effectively across diverse global teams

Clorox

- o Talent
- o Drive
- o Focus on results
- o Innovation
- o Team player
- o Leadership
- o Passion

Gillette

- o Organizational excellence
- o Achievement
- o Integrity
- o Collaboration

Microsoft

- o Long-term approach
- o Strategic thinking
- o Passion for products and technology
- o Customer focus

- o Individual excellence
- o Team spirit
- o Interpersonal skills

PepsiCo

- o Results orientation
- o Commitment to excellence
- o Willingness to learn
- o Sense of excitement
- o Ability to innovate
- o Intelligence
- o Dedication

Proctor & Gamble

- o Leadership
- o Capacity
- o Risk-taking
- o Innovation
- o Solutions
- o Collaboration
- o Mastery

SC Johnson

- o Leadership
- o High initiative
- o Analytical ability
- o Teamwork skills
- o Creativity
- o Innovation

Unilever

- o Determination to win
- o Business focus
- o Intellectual skills
- o People skills
- o Integrity

Concentration in Finance

CitiGroup

- o Integrity
- o Excellence
- o Respect
- o Teamwork
- o Ownership
- o Leadership

Deutsche Bank

- o Customer focus
- o Teamwork
- o Innovation
- o Performance
- o Trust
- o Passion to perform

Fidelity Investments

- o Understanding of the financial services industry
- o Knowledge of accounting and financial principles
- o Ability to work effectively with senior executives
- o Strong analytical skills

- o Excellent time management skills
- o Ability to organize, prioritize, and multi-task
- o Excellent project management and presentation skills

Goldman Sachs

- o Passion for excellence
- o Belief in the power of the group
- o Integrity
- o Trust
- o Leadership
- o Desire to be challenged
- o Drive

Lehman Brothers

- o Problem solving and analytic ability
- o Leadership
- o Initiative
- o Team player
- o Self confidence
- o Assertiveness
- o Maturity
- o Ability to interact with others, persuade, and listen
- o Recognition of own strengths and weaknesses

Morgan Stanley

- o Energetic
- o Creative
- o Well-rounded
- o Outgoing
- o Self-motivated

o   Ability to learn quickly

o   Strong quantitative and analytical skills

o   Desire to thrive in a dynamic, high-pressure environment

UBS Investment Bank

o   Problem analysis

o   Judgment and decision making

o   Innovation

o   Communication and impact

o   Drive and commitment

o   Teamwork

o   Planning and organizing

Notes

---

[1] This information is provided for illustration purposes only; for up-to-date information about the recruitment processes, please obtain the necessary information directly from the target companies.

Appendix B: The Résumé

The first impression you make on the recruiting company is created by your résumé. It is your résumé that gets you to the first round of interviews. Therefore, your résumé should not simply reflect your achievements to date but should also clearly indicate your value to the recruiter. Ideally, you should tailor your résumé to address the specifics of each company; however, there are several basic résumé-writing principles that apply to most recruiters. These principles are outlined below.

o   Each line on your résumé should give the interviewer a reason to hire you. This is the key to the successful résumé. Be prepared to elaborate on each point in your résumé.

o   Structure your résumé around three main categories: (1) education, (2) work experience, and (3) additional information.

o   The "education" section of your résumé should provide details of graduate work and college education. Include your degree subject, university, GPA, and any major distinctions (e.g., Magna cum laude), awards, and prizes that might help document your academic abilities. Consider explaining the importance of an award, if you think the recruiter might not be familiar with it (e.g., top 1% of students nationally). You might also include any significant academic accomplishments (e.g., thesis, major research projects) that you believe will enhance your value to the recruiter.

o   The "additional information" section of your résumé (which can also be labeled "other skills and accomplishments") should highlight any relevant experiences that demonstrate skills valued by the interviewing company, such as leadership, creativity, teamwork, management skills, and drive. To illustrate, you could include leadership positions, significant involvement in extracurricular activities, and significant accomplishments in sports. The key is to list only those activities that are likely to enhance your value proposition to the company, rather than listing them just to make your résumé longer. Include any foreign languages and rate your fluency (e.g., basic, competent, or fluent).

o   List your prior jobs (or educational experience) in reverse chronological order, starting with the most recent. Many recruiters recommend listing dates on the left hand side to provide a better overview of your background.

o   Avoid using professional jargon. Your résumé should be impressive, yet easy to understand.

o   Your résumé should be clearly laid out. Do not use creative formatting. The focus should be on the content, not on visually distracting details. Do not use fonts that are difficult to read; do not make the font size unreasonably small (e.g., to fit in more information).

Appendix C: General Interview Guidelines

Following are a number of specific issues that a candidate needs to master in order to succeed in the interview process.

Before the Interview

o   Research the industry and the company.

o   Find out how the company conducts its interviews. Boston Consulting Group and McKinsey, for example, provide detailed case analysis advice and examples on their websites.

o   Determine the value to you of working for that company. Why would you like to work for that company? This is a question to which you should know the answer, not only because it is likely to come up in the interview, but also because it will help you articulate your level of interest in the company.

o   Identify your value to the interviewing company. What is your value proposition, that is, what are the competencies and assets you bring to the company? How would you position yourself? What makes you more valuable than other candidates interviewing for the same position?

o   Be fluent with your own résumé; anticipate the likely questions and have an answer ready.

o   Be prepared to ask questions about the company, its vision, defining characteristics, working environment, the role that newly hired associates are likely to play, their likely career track, etc.

o   Practice. Do mock interviews with friends, teammates, and your school's career office; videotape your interviews and get feedback; observe others' mock interviews as well.

During the Interview

o   Be on time.

o   Always have your résumé with you, even if you expect the recruiter to have a copy.

o   Begin and end the interview with a firm handshake.

- Make good eye contact. This will help you engage the interviewer, establish rapport, and contribute to the interactivity of the interview.

- Be a good listener. Do not interrupt the interviewer when he/she is speaking. Be prepared to take notes.

- Be positive. Rather than talking about the negatives, talk about the positives. Talk about what you learned from difficult situations and how you overcame those challenges.

- Do not get personal. In most cases, it is a good idea to stay away from topics such as the interviewer's family, physical appearance, religious or political beliefs, age and ethnic background.

- Control your nervousness. Discover where your nervous energy goes (e.g., laughing, playing with your pen, tapping your fingers), and try to channel this energy into listening and responding to the interviewer's questions and comments.

- Do not ramble. Articulate your thoughts clearly and succinctly throughout the interview.

- Project confidence and be calm (even if something goes "wrong"). Your ability to work the case confidently, without getting flustered or frustrated, is paramount.

- Most important – relax and try to have fun during the interview. (Easier said than done, but you should always try to create an atmosphere that fosters easy communication between you and the interviewer).

After the Interview

- A thank-you note (letter or email) can make a difference. Send it within two days of the interview and try to make it personal. If you send notes to more than one person from the same company, expect that the notes will be shared and try to make them sound different.

- When feasible, collect feedback on your performance and use this feedback to improve for the next interview. Think about what worked and what did not. Identify areas for improvement and get additional practice in these areas.

Appendix D: The Introduction

Most interviews begin with an open-ended general question designed to break the ice and set the tone for the interview. The introduction question also gives candidates an opportunity to state their value proposition early on in the interview. Answer strategies to some of the most common introduction questions are given below.

o   Tell us about yourself.

   ▶ This is the prototypical question to start the interview. Prepare a narrative that highlights who you are and, most important, your unique value proposition to the interviewing company. You cannot avoid this question and should have a ready answer for it. In fact, even if not asked, you should still work the answer into the interview (e.g., "it might be helpful if I start by providing my background"). Prepare a one-, three-, and five-minute version of your story so that you have the option to choose the narrative that best fits the interview timeframe.

o   Walk me through your résumé and explain the decisions you have made to date (Describe your career progression to date).

   ▶ This is a straightforward question and you should be able to answer it in about two minutes, but be prepared to go into much greater depth, if asked. As you walk the interviewer through your résumé, make sure to use your accomplishments to underscore your value proposition to the company (i.e., why the company should hire you).

o   Why would you like to work for us?

   ▶ You should have an answer for this question. If you can't answer it, you should take this company off your list.

o   Why should we hire you?

   ▶ Offer a brief summary of your value proposition. Describe the key assets and competencies that you bring to the firm. You can organize them around the three key factors: skills, knowledge, and fit with the company.

o   Why did you decide to get an MBA, and why did you choose to do it at this school?

▶ Your answer should focus on your ambitions to grow professionally. Explain why the school you have chosen to attend is the best fit for you given your current skills and long-term goals.

Appendix E: Personal Experience Interview Questions

Most personal interview questions fall into one of the following areas: leadership, analytical skills, creativity, teamwork, communication skills, management skills, drive, fit with the company, interest in the interviewer's company, and interest in the functional area of marketing/consulting. Examples of such questions in each area are given below:

Leadership

o   Tell me of a time you showed leadership skills.

o   Give an example of your ability to build motivation in your co-workers, classmates, or a volunteer committee.

o   What is the toughest group that you've had to get cooperation from? Describe how you handled it. What was the outcome?

o   Describe a situation in which you recognized a problem or an opportunity. How did you respond? Did you choose to address this situation on your own? What obstacles did you face and how did you overcome them?

o   What leadership roles have you played prior to applying for a position with our company?

o   Have you ever had an idea or a goal to achieve something that required action by other people? How did you implement this idea?

o   Describe a situation in which you had to convince others that your view, approach, or ideas were right or appropriate.

o   Describe a situation in which you led a group to complete a complex assignment and motivated others to get the work done on time

o   Describe a situation in which you made a difference.

o   Describe a time when you tried to persuade another person to do something that he/she was not eager to do.

o   How would you build a team out of independent individuals?

- How do you motivate people?

- How do you help ensure that your team meets project deadlines?

- Describe a situation demonstrating your ability to foster teamwork early on and prove yourself to have the potential to become a team leader.

- How did you foster effective and open communication and achieve your and your teammates' goals?

- How did you resolve differences of opinion?

- How did you build a shared vision and shared goals?

- How did you resolve group tensions?

- How did you instill in others an atmosphere of support, responsiveness, and respect?

- What was the most challenging group you successfully worked with?

- Describe a situation in which you were in charge of a group of people and moved something forward. How did you mobilize the team to work toward achieving the result you chose?

Analytical Skills

- Tell me about your analytical skills.

- You seem to have strong analytical skills. Why do you believe that you can handle the requirements of the job you are applying for?

- Tell me about a complex problem you had to solve, and walk me through your thinking as you solved it.

- Describe a situation in which you took a complex problem and designed an actionable strategy to solve this problem.

- Describe a situation in which you had to make an important decision without having all the necessary information at hand.

- How would you describe your approach to solving problems?

o Describe a situation in which you had to apply your skills to learn a new technology or a process.

Creativity

o In your work experience, what have you done that you consider truly creative?

o How would you define creativity?

o Would your friends/colleagues describe you as a creative person?

o Tell me about a creative solution that you developed for a difficult problem.

o Describe a situation in which you developed a unique and resourceful solution to a difficult problem.

o Describe a situation that demonstrates your ability to see multiple options or look at things from a different point of view.

o Which of your creative accomplishments has given you the most satisfaction?

Teamwork

o How would your team members describe you?

o Describe a recent unpopular decision you made and the results of this decision.

o Do you prefer to work by yourself or with others?

o What makes for a good team member?

o What types of people do you have trouble getting along with?

o Tell me three positive and three negative things your team members would say about your interactions with them.

o What experiences have you had working in teams? What were the most (least) satisfying aspects of working on that team? How do you determine the role you play on the team? What is the most difficult thing for you in working with your team members?

o What makes you most effective with people? What kinds of people do you find most challenging? What conflicts or difficulties do you experience?

o Describe a specific experience working in a group or team situation where there was interpersonal conflict. Describe how you approached the conflict, what worked well, and what did not. How did you manage the outcome?

Communication Skills

o Tell me about a situation in which you had to speak up or be assertive in order to get an important point across.

o How would you define good communication skills?

o How would you rate your communication skills? What have you done to improve them?

o Describe a time when you had to change your communication style to deliver a message or get your point across.

o Describe the most important document, report, or presentation that you had to complete.

o Give me some examples of how you have adapted your own communicating style to deal with different people and situations.

o Would you rather write a report or give a verbal report? Why?

o How would you rate your writing abilities? Your listening skills?

o Describe a situation in which you experienced ineffective communication. What would you do differently in this situation?

o Sell me this pen (bottle of water, computer, etc.).

Management Skills

o Give an example of what you've done when your time schedule or project plan was upset by unforeseen circumstances.

o Tell me about a recent crisis you handled.

- Give an example of when you had to settle a dispute between two individuals.

- Do you work well under pressure?

- Can you make fast decisions?

- Do you manage your time well?

- How do you handle different priorities in your life (e.g., family, work, school, sports)?

- How do you make important decisions?

- How do you manage risk?

- What do you do when you are having trouble with a project?

- What was your most difficult decision in the last six months? What made it difficult?

- Your boss (client) tells you to do something you believe is wrong. What do you do?

- Describe your management philosophy.

- Describe a situation in which you had to make an important decision without having all the necessary information at hand.

- Describe a situation demonstrating your ability to transition quickly and effectively to different tasks.

- How did you shift priorities and modify actions to meet changing job demands on short notice?

- How did you prepare for this interview?

Capacity to Learn

- Describe a difficult situation that you feel you should have handled differently. What did you learn from that experience?

- You have had little experience with marketing (finance, technology, etc.). How do you intend to learn what is required from the position you are applying for?

- How do you handle change?

- Are your grades a good measure of your ability to learn?

- o If hired, you will be working with experienced individuals who have been with the company for many years. What makes you think that your performance will be at par with theirs?

- o In what areas do you need to develop professionally? How do you plan to achieve that?

Drive

- o Give me examples of projects or tasks you started on your own.

- o Give me an example of how you demonstrated initiative.

- o What are you most important long-term goals? What aspirations do you have for yourself over the next five or so years — professionally and personally?

- o Where do you see yourself in two (five, ten) years?

- o What does "success" ("failure") mean to you?

- o Describe a situation in which you aspired to reach a goal. What obstacles confronted you along the way? What did you do to overcome them?

- o Tell me about a time you hit a wall trying to push forward a great idea.

- o Describe a situation that demanded sustained, unusually hard work, where others might have thought you couldn't succeed. Was the experience stressful? If so, how did you handle the stress?

Company Fit

- o What experiences/skills do you feel are particularly transferable to our organization?

- o What type of work do you like to do best?

- o What accomplishments have given you the greatest satisfaction?

- o Describe one of your most defining experiences.

- o What was the most important thing your parents (prior job experiences) taught you?

o   Other than money, what makes you happy at work?

o   If you could have dinner with anyone, dead or alive, who would it be and why?

o   How do you spend your spare time? What is your favorite hobby? What is a recent book you read? A movie you saw?

o   Have you heard anything about our company that you do not like?

o   How would you fit with our corporate culture?

o   What do you consider more important, a high salary or career advancement?

o   What characteristics should we be looking for in the "ideal" candidate for our company?

Interest in the Functional Area

o   Why would you like to pursue a career in consulting (marketing)?

o   Why are you interested in marketing/brand management?

o   What brands do you feel passionately about and why?

o   Which three items would you take with you to "Brand Manager Island"?

Interest in the Company

o   Why would you choose our firm over our competitors?

o   Why do you want to work for our company?

o   How long do you plan to stay with our company?

o   Is there anything that will prevent you from taking a position with our company?

o   With what other firms are you interviewing?

o   Which other industries are you looking into?

o   Which of our company's products would you like to market? Why?

o   Who is our main competitor?

o   How would you improve the performance of our company?

o Where do you think our industry is going? What are the
   key trends and how would they impact our company?

Appendix F: Strengths, Weaknesses, and Mistakes

Some of the most common interview questions involve asking candidates to identify their strengths, weaknesses, successes, and mistakes. Examples of such questions and possible answer strategies are given below.

o   Identify your key strengths.

▶ This is an easy question for most candidates. The key issue here is to underscore the strengths that fit the company needs.

⊹ Variations of the same question:

– What makes you special?

– How would you describe yourself? Name three adjectives that describe you best.

– How would your friends (teammates, boss) describe you?

– If you had a blank billboard on which to create an ad for yourself, how would you fill the billboard?

– If you created an advertisement for yourself for this position, what would it be like?

– Which brand best fits your personality and why? Describe your strengths and how you would position yourself in the marketplace.

o   Identify your key weaknesses.

▶ This is a difficult, as well as a very tricky, question. Everyone has weaknesses, but you do not want them to hinder your chance of getting an offer. There is no common approach to this question; however, it is important to have a ready answer.

As a general rule, you might consider not emphasizing weaknesses that reflect a major deficiency in the skills required for the position you are applying for, weaknesses that could potentially result in significant damage (e.g., financial loss, negative publicity, loss of a client) to your employer, and weaknesses for which you cannot clearly articulate how you intend to successfully overcome their potential limitations – and ultimately convert these weaknesses into strengths.

One possible answer strategy when talking about your weaknesses is to state that you have no shortcomings that will prevent you from doing an excellent job and being an asset to your interviewer's company. An alternative strategy is to put a positive spin on the question: Instead of talking about weaknesses, identify areas in which you are likely to perform your best (which implicitly identifies some areas in which you might not be that strong). In most cases, it is a good idea to avoid clichés of the type: "I work too much."

Overall, it is important to keep in mind that selectively identifying your weaknesses has important ethical implications. Thus, if you think that you have major deficiencies, instead of hiding them from your employer, you should consider working on them to improve your performance prior to the interview.

o   What are your three (two, one) most important accomplishments? Why?

▶ This is a straightforward question: Pick accomplishments that most clearly communicate your value to the company.

o   What is your greatest failure?

▶ This is another difficult question requiring a well-thought-out answer. The goal is to identify a failure that does not hinder your chance of getting an offer. In general, you might want to avoid failures that resulted in a significant damage (e.g., financial loss, negative publicity, loss of a client) to your employer, failures that reflect a major deficiency in the skills required for the position you are applying for, failures that are too recent and from which you have not had a chance to learn from, as well as failures for which you cannot clearly articulate the lessons learned and provide an example of a scenario in which you successfully resolved a similar problem.

One strategy to address this question is to embed your failure in a context that turns this failure into a valuable experience. This approach, summarized in Figure 10, calls for a brief description of the failure, which is then followed by a summary of the lessons learned from that experience and a success story demonstrating how you applied the lessons learned from the failure to your advantage. Conclude your story by identifying how the lessons learned from your failure enhances your value to the company.

Figure 10: Framing a Failure as a Learning Experience

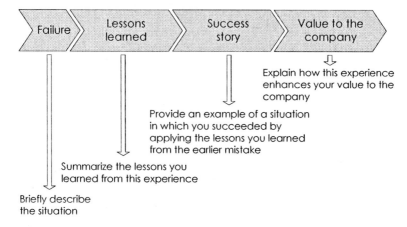

Explain how this experience enhances your value to the company

Provide an example of a situation in which you succeeded by applying the lessons you learned from the earlier mistake

Summarize the lessons you learned from this experience

Briefly describe the situation

Appendix G: Concluding Questions

At the end of the interview most recruiters let candidates ask questions. The goal of these questions is twofold. First, they aim to provide candidates with additional information about the company, its current projects, culture, and work environment. Second, the questions candidates ask are also a part of the interview. They are used to evaluate candidates' interest in the company, their goals, priorities, and value system. Examples of two typical end-of-the-interview questions and answer strategies are given below.

o   Do you have any questions for us?

▶ If this is a company you would like to work for, you most likely will have questions. The most common areas for questions include the company's vision for the future, your role in the company (short term and long term), the company's culture, your prospects for growth within the company, and current projects that the company is working on. The questions you ask reflect your priorities, so ask about things that are really important to you.

o   Is there anything you would like to add (anything else we should know about you)?

▶ This question gives you the opportunity to summarize your value proposition to the company. You can answer this question the same way you would answer the question "Why should we hire you?" Describe the key assets and competencies that you bring to the firm. You can organize them around the three key factors: skills, knowledge, and fit with the company.

Appendix H: The Language of Action and Success

Your personal experience stories should project a winning management style: They should reflect the nature of the problem, the actions you have taken, and the outcome of these actions. Describing your prior experience calls for using active language to effectively communicate your unique contribution to each project. A number of common action phrases used in résumé writing and during the interview to communicate your achievement are given below:

- o Accelerated [performance, development, customer acquisition]

- o Accomplished [project, goal, task]

- o Achieved a goal

- o Administered [contract, project, task]

- o Aligned [people to a goal, goal and strategy, strategy and tactics]

- o Analyzed [financial impact, organizational fit]

- o Assessed [risk, impact, competitive threat, market forces]

- o Assisted [senior management, clients]

- o Bridged a gap

- o Capitalized on an opportunity

- o Collected, analyzed, and reported market data

- o Completed the project [on schedule, under budget]

- o Conceived [idea, strategy, project]

- o Conducted [financial, marketing, competitive, sensitivity] analysis

- o Coordinated communications to internal and external [constituencies, stakeholders, entities]

- o Coordinated team efforts

- o Created a vision

- o Defined [scope, strategy, implementation plan]
- o Designed [strategy, tactics, implementation plan]
- o Developed [strategy, marketing plan, vision]
- o Devised [program, strategy, project]
- o Directed [project, employees, program]
- o Established [guidelines, benchmarks, goals]
- o Estimated [market potential, competitive response]
- o Evaluated new business opportunities
- o Evaluated market reaction to [promotions, advertising, price]
- o Exceeded a goal
- o Executed [strategy, business plan]
- o Expanded [operation, project, scope]
- o Facilitated [process, acquisition, implementation]
- o Formulated [hypotheses, strategy, action plan]
- o Fostered collaboration
- o Generated new ideas
- o Identified [strategic gap, opportunities, alternatives, strategies]
- o Implemented [program, strategy, goals]
- o Improved [communications, customer satisfaction, morale, performance]
- o Increased [profits, revenues, sales volume]
- o Initiated [project, activity, policy]
- o Interacted with [clients, project management, stakeholders]
- o Led [product management team, cross-functional teams]
- o Managed [project/cross-functional team, the development and implementation of a strategic plan]
- o Modified program

- Motivated [team, employees, stakeholders]
- Negotiated [deal, settlement, acquisition]
- Optimized [business model, resource allocation policy, operating structure]
- Outlined [strategy, vision, project]
- Persuaded [clients, management]
- Planned [mergers, strategies, projects]
- Prepared client reports
- Presented [analysis, recommendations, solutions]
- Produced [results, projects, goals]
- Rebuilt [infrastructure, confidence, strategies]
- Reduced [costs, exposure, vulnerability, response time, turnaround time, turnover, uncertainty]
- Resolved a conflict
- Responded to a crisis
- Responsible for [new product development, strategic planning, customer management, project, team, new client development, client account]
- Set goals
- Solved a problem
- Streamlined [process, operations, policy]
- Strengthened [reputation, performance]
- Structured [new venture, deal]
- Surpassed [requirements, goals, projections]
- Took [a risk, initiative]
- Won [award, contract, competition]

Appendix I: Functional Knowledge Questions

Functional knowledge questions reflect the basic business terminology, principles, frameworks, and theories that are essential in the context of a particular functional area (e.g., marketing, accounting, finance, and consulting). There are two basic types of functional knowledge questions: questions probing your theoretical knowledge (e.g., frameworks, models, and concepts) and questions calling for specific examples to illustrate a particular concept. Examples of common interview questions from each of these two types are given below.

Conceptual Questions

o   What is a unique value proposition?

o   You're launching a new product line for our company. Walk me through your decision on how to structure pricing (advertising, distribution, service).

o   Which of the four Ps is the most important?

o   A brand is very powerful in one product category of the supermarket. How do you determine whether to leverage the brand in another category? (i.e., Should Coke enter the ice cream market?)

o   How do you determine whether or not to do a line extension?

o   If your brand manager asks you to write a marketing plan for the next year, what would the table of contents look like?

o   Which is more profitable, a 10% increase in price or a 10% increase in share?

o   What is brand equity?

o   What is conjoint analysis? When would you use it?

o   What would you do to double a company's market share?

o   If you were a cab driver in a new city, how would you become the most profitable cab driver in that city?

- What are the 10 most important questions that you would ask to find out about a brand on your first day of work as a brand manager?
- How do you define marketing (consulting)?
- You are the brand manager of Company X and you need a new product to drive the top line. Where do you go?
- How would you evaluate the success of an advertising campaign?
- Is Super Bowl advertising a good value?

Example Questions

- Name a product you think is marketed (advertised) well.
- Identify one good and one bad commercial.
- Identify a website that markets consumer goods well.
- Identify a brand that you feel is (is not) marketed well. Why is it (isn't it) marketed well?
- Tell me about a new product introduction you liked. What would you have done differently to market the product?
- Tell me about a poor product that was marketed well. What would you have done differently to the product?
- Identify a product/company that has made a huge strategic error. Why was it an error?

Appendix J: Winning Case Interview Strategies

Mastering the case analysis requires the ability to deal creatively with complex problems and to reach logical conclusions, based on the available information, in a short period of time. The case interview also calls for strong communication, teamwork, and general management skills because the interactive nature of case analysis adds a dynamic dimension to the interview by letting the recruiter observe your poise, self-confidence, and communication skills under pressure. A set of winning strategies on how to manage these two aspects of the case interview are outlined below.

Solving the Case

o   Make sure you are answering the question you have been asked; ask questions if you are unsure about the details. Misunderstanding the question or answering the wrong question is one of the most common mistakes in a case interview.

o   Remember that rarely are you given all the case information up front. You are expected to ask intelligent questions that will reveal the relevant information that is not readily available.

o   Be systematic. Finish one key question and summarize the findings before you go on to the next. Step back periodically to summarize what you have learned so far and how it relates to the problem you are trying to solve. Do not proceed in a haphazard fashion, jumping from one issue to another.

o   Use frameworks creatively. Do not force-fit a familiar framework to a problem (one of the most common case analysis mistakes). The key is to use common sense.

o   Always focus on the big picture: Solve the problem without getting stuck in details. Prioritize issues. Start with factors that are likely to have the greatest impact. There is no need to mention the framework you will be using by name; instead, explain the structure of your analysis so that the interviewer understands your thought process.

o   Stay away from phrases like "as we learned in our strategy class..." and "the textbook says that..." to justify your decisions. You should be able on your own to explain and justify the logic for your arguments.

o Do not be afraid to think "outside the box." There is no box. Creativity and brainstorming may be just what the interviewer is looking for. Use business judgment, logic, and common sense.

o Identify the assumptions you are making to solve the problem. Explain the rationale for making these assumptions and their consistency with the facts of the case. Always clarify whether you are making assumptions of your own or restating the case facts.

o When possible, use visual aids to support your analysis. Use flowcharts to represent business processes (e.g., the value delivery process); use bullet points to identify different case points (e.g., facts, assumptions, and logical arguments); use matrixes to represent more complex relationships between factors with multiple levels (e.g., product-market matrix).

o When possible, use calculations to support your analysis. This is an opportunity to demonstrate your quantitative skills.

Interacting with the Interviewer

o Listen carefully and take notes. Remember that you are not expected to have a ready solution to the case problem; take a moment to collect your thoughts.

o Think out loud. The interviewer wants to know your thought process, not just the solution. If you have rejected some alternatives, explain why so that the interviewer has a better understanding of your thought process.

o Structure your answer by explaining your strategy (framework) up front so that the interviewer knows what you are trying to do.

o Be confident, even if you do not know the answer to a specific question. It is important for the interviewer to understand that you know how to react if a client asks you something you do not know.

o   Remember that "cracking the case" does not mean finding the "right" answer (which rarely exists). It is all about how you analyze the problem.

o   Interact with the interviewer. The case should be a dialogue, not a monologue.

o   Be flexible in defending your point. The interviewer might disagree with you to test your reaction to being challenged. Keep an open mind and watch for cues from the interviewer.

o   Think of the interviewer as a teammate and the case as a client assignment. The interview is a test of your ability to interact with your teammates and clients.

o   Have fun. Interviewers are looking for people who enjoy solving problems and are fun to work with. Think of case analysis as an opportunity to discuss novel ideas and address challenging problems with smart people.

Remember that the best way to ensure that all of the above issues come to you naturally during the interview is to practice. Practice solving different cases to become more comfortable with the process.

Appendix K: Business Cases

Depending on the nature of the underlying problem, most business cases can be classified as either action-based or problem-based. Action-based cases deal with situations in which the company is considering a specific strategic action (e.g., launching a new product, repositioning an existing product, entering new markets, acquiring or merging with another company). In contrast, problem-based cases involve optimizing the performance of an existing business program rather than developing a new program. These cases are typically defined either by the presence of a performance gap (e.g., declining profitability, revenues, market share) or by a change in the environment in which the company operates (e.g., a new competitive entry, a competitive action, changes in customer demand, changes in technology, legal regulations, and government policies). Examples of common interview questions for each of these types of cases are given below.

Action-Based Cases

o You are charged with marketing, in the United States, a candy bar that has been very successful in France. What things should you consider in bringing the product to market in the United States?

o Your client is trying to decide whether or not to invest in an office equipment company. You have been asked to assess the long-term attractiveness of the office equipment market.

o Your client must build a new computer chip manufacturing plant. You must decide which country to build the plant in. What factors would you consider?

o Your client is considering launching a new product. Market data show that launching the product will decrease sales of an existing product by x%. Do you launch the product?

o R&D comes up with a new formula to revitalize your product. What questions would you ask to evaluate this improvement?

o A department store in Chicago is buying an equally prestigious department store in another city and changing that store's name to match its own. How do you handle changing the name of the store that meant so much to the other city? What do you do?

o Develop an advertising campaign for product x.

Problem-Based Cases: Performance Gaps

o Your market share has been declining for the past year. What would you do?

o Your client would like to increase its profit margins by 6%. What would be your advice?

o You are a product manager for product X. For the past few years, the market share of your company has been decreasing even though the overall category was flat. What would you do?

o You are the brand manager for a product whose sales have been flat for the last five years. However, the brand's market share has been growing by 5% per year. What is going on with the brand, and what would you do about it?

o Your brand has experienced substantial share erosion for the past several years because of a competitor that claims to be "better." Under what circumstances should you reformulate your product?

o A company's market share is decreasing and the two options on the table are to lower the price or to advertise. What would you do?

Problem-Based Cases: Changes in the Environment

o Your competitor just lowered its price. What do you do?

o Your competitor just launched an aggressive advertising campaign. What do you do?

o What would you do if R&D told you that they have come up with a pasta sauce that lowers cholesterol?

o How should Fatburger (fast food chain) react to consumers' obsession with fat-free food?

o How should Segway react to state laws restricting the use of Segways on sidewalks?

Appendix L: Estimation Cases

Estimation cases are a form of brainteasers commonly given in interviews to test candidates' logical thinking and observe their quantitative skills. Examples of estimation questions given at management interviews are offered below.

Question: How many golf balls does it take to fill up an Olympic swimming pool?

Solution A: The popular solution is to compare the volume of the swimming pool and the golf ball. Given that the pool is 50 meters x 25 meters x 3 meters, its volume is 3,750 cubic meters, or 228,837,667 cubic inches. The golf ball's volume is 2.48 cubic inches (the radius of the golf ball is 0.84 inches and the formula for measuring the volume of a sphere is: [4 x (Pi) x radius cubed] / 3). Given that the densest packing of spheres possible is 74%, it can be calculated that it takes 68.28 million golf balls to fill the pool. Note, however, that this solution requires very specific knowledge (e.g., the formula for measuring the volume of a sphere and the maximum density packing coefficient) and, hence, is not readily applicable to most MBA interviews.

Solution B: An alternative (and more intuitive) solution does not require knowing complex formulas. The size of an Olympic pool is 50 meters x 25 meters x 3 meters. The diameter of a golf ball is 1.68 inches or .0427 meters (1 inch = 2.54 centimeters). Therefore, it will take 685,000 golf balls to cover the bottom of the pool (1,171 x 585). The depth of the pool is 3 meters or 70 golf balls. Therefore, when golf balls are stacked up by putting each layer precisely on top of one another, the swimming pool will accommodate approximately 47.95 million balls (685,000 x 70). Note, however that a greater efficiency can be achieved by shifting every other layer by 2.1 centimeters (half a golf ball). Assume that it will result in approximately 40% stacking efficiency (which can be illustrated by a simple drawing) – that is, instead of 70 layers of golf balls the pool will accommodate 98 layers (70 x 1.4). Therefore, the total amount of balls the swimming pool can accommodate is about 67.13 million (685,000 x 98).

Question: How many barbers are there in Chicago?

Solution: Chicago's population is close to 3 million → assume 50% are men → assume 6 haircuts per year → 9 million haircuts per year. Assume also that each haircut takes 30 minutes and the average barber works 8 hours a day, 5 days a week, 50 weeks a year (2 weeks vacation) → 4,000 haircuts per year. Therefore, there should be 2,250 barbers (assuming that all men get a haircut from a barber; if this is not the case, then the derived number is overestimated).

Additional Estimation Questions:

- o What is the size of the restaurant market in Chicago?

- o How many computers are sold daily?

- o What is the weight of a Boeing 747?

- o How many gas stations (pay phones, restaurants) are there in Chicago?

- o How would you go about estimating your competitor's budget for advertising/promotional/R&D expenses?

- o How many car batteries are sold in the United States each year?

Appendix M: Logic Cases

Logic cases are a form of brainteaser cases commonly given in interviews to test candidates' ability to deal with abstract problems and to observe their problem-solving process. Examples of logic problems given at management interviews are offered below.

Problem: Why are manhole covers round?

Solution A: A round cover cannot fall into a manhole, whereas square or rectangular ones can (e.g., if placed diagonally).

Solution B: Round manhole covers are easier to be rolled down the street if necessary.

Problem: Why do Coke cans have an indent at the bottom?

Solution: To control can expansion so that, in case of pressure, it does not bulge in the opposite direction or at the sides, which would not allow the can to stand up normally and would make it less visually appealing.

Problem: You are in a room with three light switches. Each one controls one light bulb in the next room. Your goal is to figure out which switch controls which light bulb. You may flick only two switches and may enter into the light bulb room only once.

Solution: The key is to realize that a light bulb can also be tested by touch. Flick the first switch, wait for a few minutes, then turn it off and flick the second switch. Enter the light bulb room. The bulb that is on connects to the second switch. The warm light bulb is controlled by the first switch.

Problem: Consider a set of cards, each one having a letter on one side and a number on the other side. You are given a subset of four cards as follows (the upper side): D-K-3-7. You have to test the following rule: If a card has a D on one side, it has a 3 on the other side. You must decide which cards need to be turned over to know whether this sample of cards is consistent with the rule.

Solution: The correct cards are D and 7 (although 90% of people pick D and 3). Seeing what is on the reverse of the 7 card can lead to disconfirming the rule if a D shows up (whereas seeing what is on the reverse of the 3 card cannot disconfirm the rule and is, hence, non-informative).[1]

Problem: Suppose that there are four possible kinds of objects: (1) an unhappy dodecahedron, (2) a happy dodecahedron, (3) an unhappy cube, and (4) a happy cube. Suppose, as well, that I have written down on a hidden piece of paper one of the attitudes (unhappy or happy) and one of the shapes (dodecahedron or cube). Now read the following rule carefully: An object is a GOKE if, and only if, it has either the attitude I have written down, or the shape I have written down, but not both. I will tell you that the unhappy dodecahedron is a GOKE. Which of the other objects, if any, is a GOKE?

Solution: A happy cube.[2]

Problem: A bat and a ball cost $1.10 in total. The bat costs $1 more than the ball. How much does the ball cost?

Solution: The ball costs five cents.[3]

Notes

[1] Wason, P. C. (1960), "On the Failure to Eliminate Hypotheses in a Conceptual Task," *Quarterly Journal of Experimental Psychology*, 12, 129-140.
[2] Ibid.
[3] Kahneman, Daniel (2003), "Maps of Bounded Rationality: Psychology for Behavioral Economics Dagger," *American Economic Review*, 93, 1449.

Author Profile

Alexander Chernev is associate professor of marketing at the Kellogg School of Management, Northwestern University, where he teaches the core marketing management course to MBA students and behavioral decision theory to Ph.D. students. He holds a Ph.D. in Psychology from Sofia University and a Ph.D. in Business Administration from Duke University. Professor Chernev's research applies theories and concepts related to consumer behavior and managerial decision making to develop successful corporate branding and customer management strategies. His research has been published in the leading marketing journals and he has received numerous teaching and research awards. Professor Chernev serves on the editorial boards of the *Journal of Consumer Research* and the *Journal of Consumer Psychology* and has advised numerous companies on issues such as strategic marketing, new product development, and customer management. Professor Chernev has provided career advice to numerous students, many of whom are currently working for Fortune 500 companies and others who are in the process of building their own Fortune 500 companies.

The Kellogg School of Management was ranked by *Business Week* as the number one graduate school of business in the United States, an honor it has achieved a record five times since the inception of the survey. It was also was named the top MBA program in the world for the third consecutive year by the Economist Intelligence Unit. Both *Business Week* and *U.S. News and World Report* have named the Kellogg School as the number one executive MBA program for more than a decade. The Marketing Department at the Kellogg School of Management has been consistently rated the top marketing department in the United States and worldwide by all major surveys.

Printed in the United States
36102LVS00002B/339-362

9 780976 306122